Welcome Baby

Stick your favorite picture here

Guest

My Predictions

Baby's date of birth

Time of birth

Hours of labor

Baby weight

Baby height

Hair color

Eye color

Name suggestion

First word

Advice for Parents

Wishes for Baby

Guest

My Predictions

Baby's date of birth

Time of birth

Hours of labor

Baby weight

Baby height

Hair color

Eye color

Name suggestion

First word

Advice for Parents

Wishes for Baby

Guest

My Predictions

Baby's date of birth

Time of birth

Hours of labor

Baby weight

Baby height

Hair color

Eye color

Name suggestion

First word

Advice for Parents

Wishes for Baby

Guest

My Predictions

Baby's date of birth　　　Time of birth　　　Hours of labor

Baby weight　　　Baby height

Hair color　　　Eye color

Name suggestion　　　First word

Advice for Parents

Wishes for Baby

Guest

My Predictions

Baby's date of birth   Time of birth   Hours of labor

Baby weight   Baby height

Hair color   Eye color

Name suggestion   First word

Advice for Parents

Wishes for Baby

Guest

My Predictions

Baby's date of birth

Time of birth

Hours of labor

Baby weight

Baby height

Hair color

Eye color

Name suggestion

First word

Advice for Parents

Wishes for Baby

Guest

My Predictions

Baby's date of birth   Time of birth   Hours of labor

Baby weight   Baby height

Hair color   Eye color

Name suggestion   First word

Advice for Parents

Wishes for Baby

Guest

My Predictions

Baby's date of birth   Time of birth   Hours of labor

Baby weight   Baby height

Hair color   Eye color

Name suggestion   First word

Advice for Parents

_____
_____

Wishes for Baby

_____
_____

Guest

My Predictions

Baby's date of birth

Time of birth

Hours of labor

Baby weight

Baby height

Hair color

Eye color

Name suggestion

First word

Advice for Parents

Wishes for Baby

Guest

My Predictions

Baby's date of birth   Time of birth   Hours of labor

Baby weight   Baby height

Hair color   Eye color

Name suggestion   First word

Advice for Parents

Wishes for Baby

Guest

My Predictions

Baby's date of birth   Time of birth   Hours of labor

Baby weight   Baby height

Hair color   Eye color

Name suggestion   First word

Advice for Parents

Wishes for Baby

Guest

My Predictions

Baby's date of birth

Time of birth

Hours of labor

Baby weight

Baby height

Hair color

Eye color

Name suggestion

First word

Advice for Parents

Wishes for Baby

Guest

My Predictions

Baby's date of birth

Time of birth

Hours of labor

Baby weight

Baby height

Hair color

Eye color

Name suggestion

First word

Advice for Parents

Wishes for Baby

Guest

My Predictions

Baby's date of birth

Time of birth

Hours of labor

Baby weight

Baby height

Hair color

Eye color

Name suggestion

First word

Advice for Parents

Wishes for Baby

Guest

My Predictions

Baby's date of birth   Time of birth   Hours of labor

Baby weight   Baby height

Hair color   Eye color

Name suggestion   First word

Advice for Parents

Wishes for Baby

Guest

My Predictions

Baby's date of birth

Time of birth

Hours of labor

Baby weight

Baby height

Hair color

Eye color

Name suggestion

First word

Advice for Parents

Wishes for Baby

Guest

My Predictions

Baby's date of birth Time of birth Hours of labor

Baby weight Baby height

Hair color Eye color

Name suggestion First word

Advice for Parents

Wishes for Baby

Guest

My Predictions

Baby's date of birth

Time of birth

Hours of labor

Baby weight

Baby height

Hair color

Eye color

Name suggestion

First word

Advice for Parents

Wishes for Baby

Guest

My Predictions

Baby's date of birth

Time of birth

Hours of labor

Baby weight

Baby height

Hair color

Eye color

Name suggestion

First word

Advice for Parents

Wishes for Baby

Guest

My Predictions

Baby's date of birth

Time of birth

Hours of labor

Baby weight

Baby height

Hair color

Eye color

Name suggestion

First word

Advice for Parents

Wishes for Baby

Guest

My Predictions

Baby's date of birth

Time of birth

Hours of labor

Baby weight

Baby height

Hair color

Eye color

Name suggestion

First word

Advice for Parents

Wishes for Baby

Guest

My Predictions

Baby's date of birth Time of birth Hours of labor

Baby weight Baby height

Hair color Eye color

Name suggestion First word

Advice for Parents

_____
_____

Wishes for Baby

_____
_____

Guest

My Predictions

Baby's date of birth

Time of birth

Hours of labor

Baby weight

Baby height

Hair color

Eye color

Name suggestion

First word

Advice for Parents

Wishes for Baby

Guest

My Predictions

Baby's date of birth   Time of birth   Hours of labor

Baby weight   Baby height

Hair color   Eye color

Name suggestion   First word

Advice for Parents

Wishes for Baby

Guest

My Predictions

Baby's date of birth

Time of birth

Hours of labor

Baby weight

Baby height

Hair color

Eye color

Name suggestion

First word

Advice for Parents

Wishes for Baby

Guest

My Predictions

Baby's date of birth

Time of birth

Hours of labor

Baby weight

Baby height

Hair color

Eye color

Name suggestion

First word

Advice for Parents

_____

_____

Wishes for Baby

_____

_____

Guest

My Predictions

Baby's date of birth Time of birth Hours of labor

Baby weight Baby height

Hair color Eye color

Name suggestion First word

Advice for Parents

Wishes for Baby

Guest

My Predictions

Baby's date of birth

Time of birth

Hours of labor

Baby weight

Baby height

Hair color

Eye color

Name suggestion

First word

Advice for Parents

_____

_____

Wishes for Baby

_____

_____

Guest

_____

My Predictions

Baby's date of birthTime of birthHours of labor

Baby weightBaby height

Hair colorEye color

Name suggestionFirst word

Advice for Parents

_____
_____

Wishes for Baby

_____
_____

Guest

My Predictions

Baby's date of birth　　　　Time of birth　　　　Hours of labor

Baby weight　　　　　　　Baby height

Hair color　　　　　　　　Eye color

Name suggestion　　　　　First word

Advice for Parents

_____
_____

Wishes for Baby

_____
_____

Guest

My Predictions

Baby's date of birth　　　　Time of birth　　　　Hours of labor

Baby weight　　　　　　　　Baby height

Hair color　　　　　　　　　Eye color

Name suggestion　　　　　　First word

Advice for Parents

Wishes for Baby

Guest

My Predictions

Baby's date of birth

Time of birth

Hours of labor

Baby weight

Baby height

Hair color

Eye color

Name suggestion

First word

Advice for Parents

_____
_____

Wishes for Baby

_____
_____

Guest

My Predictions

Baby's date of birth

Time of birth

Hours of labor

Baby weight

Baby height

Hair color

Eye color

Name suggestion

First word

Advice for Parents

Wishes for Baby

Guest

My Predictions

Baby's date of birth

Time of birth

Hours of labor

Baby weight

Baby height

Hair color

Eye color

Name suggestion

First word

Advice for Parents

Wishes for Baby

Guest

My Predictions

Baby's date of birth

Time of birth

Hours of labor

Baby weight

Baby height

Hair color

Eye color

Name suggestion

First word

Advice for Parents

Wishes for Baby

Guest

My Predictions

Baby's date of birth

Time of birth

Hours of labor

Baby weight

Baby height

Hair color

Eye color

Name suggestion

First word

Advice for Parents

Wishes for Baby

Guest

My Predictions

Baby's date of birth   Time of birth   Hours of labor

Baby weight   Baby height

Hair color   Eye color

Name suggestion   First word

Advice for Parents

Wishes for Baby

Guest

My Predictions

Baby's date of birth

Time of birth

Hours of labor

Baby weight

Baby height

Hair color

Eye color

Name suggestion

First word

Advice for Parents

Wishes for Baby

Guest

My Predictions

Baby's date of birth   Time of birth   Hours of labor

Baby weight   Baby height

Hair color   Eye color

Name suggestion   First word

Advice for Parents

Wishes for Baby

Guest

My Predictions

Baby's date of birth

Time of birth

Hours of labor

Baby weight

Baby height

Hair color

Eye color

Name suggestion

First word

Advice for Parents

Wishes for Baby

Guest

_____

My Predictions

Baby's date of birth		Time of birth		Hours of labor

Baby weight			Baby height

Hair color			Eye color

Name suggestion			First word

Advice for Parents

_____
_____

Wishes for Baby

_____
_____

Guest

_____

My Predictions

Baby's date of birth   Time of birth   Hours of labor

Baby weight   Baby height

Hair color   Eye color

Name suggestion   First word

Advice for Parents

_____
_____

Wishes for Baby

_____
_____

Guest

My Predictions

Baby's date of birth

Time of birth

Hours of labor

Baby weight

Baby height

Hair color

Eye color

Name suggestion

First word

Advice for Parents

Wishes for Baby

Guest

_____

My Predictions

Baby's date of birth   Time of birth   Hours of labor

Baby weight   Baby height

Hair color   Eye color

Name suggestion   First word

Advice for Parents

_____
_____

Wishes for Baby

_____
_____

Guest

My Predictions

Baby's date of birth   Time of birth   Hours of labor

Baby weight   Baby height

Hair color   Eye color

Name suggestion   First word

Advice for Parents

Wishes for Baby

Guest

My Predictions

Baby's date of birth

Time of birth

Hours of labor

Baby weight

Baby height

Hair color

Eye color

Name suggestion

First word

Advice for Parents

Wishes for Baby

Guest

My Predictions

Baby's date of birth　　　Time of birth　　　Hours of labor

Baby weight　　　Baby height

Hair color　　　Eye color

Name suggestion　　　First word

Advice for Parents

Wishes for Baby

Guest

My Predictions

Baby's date of birth

Time of birth

Hours of labor

Baby weight

Baby height

Hair color

Eye color

Name suggestion

First word

Advice for Parents

Wishes for Baby

Guest

_____

My Predictions

Baby's date of birth   Time of birth   Hours of labor

Baby weight   Baby height

Hair color   Eye color

Name suggestion   First word

Advice for Parents

_____
_____

Wishes for Baby

_____
_____

Guest

My Predictions

Baby's date of birth

Time of birth

Hours of labor

Baby weight

Baby height

Hair color

Eye color

Name suggestion

First word

Advice for Parents

_____
_____

Wishes for Baby

_____
_____

Guest

My Predictions

Baby's date of birth

Time of birth

Hours of labor

Baby weight

Baby height

Hair color

Eye color

Name suggestion

First word

Advice for Parents

Wishes for Baby

Guest

_____

My Predictions

Baby's date of birth   Time of birth   Hours of labor

Baby weight   Baby height

Hair color   Eye color

Name suggestion   First word

Advice for Parents

_____

_____

Wishes for Baby

_____

_____

Guest

My Predictions

Baby's date of birth   Time of birth   Hours of labor

Baby weight   Baby height

Hair color   Eye color

Name suggestion   First word

Advice for Parents

Wishes for Baby

Guest

My Predictions

Baby's date of birth   Time of birth   Hours of labor

Baby weight   Baby height

Hair color   Eye color

Name suggestion   First word

Advice for Parents

Wishes for Baby

Guest

My Predictions

Baby's date of birth

Time of birth

Hours of labor

Baby weight

Baby height

Hair color

Eye color

Name suggestion

First word

Advice for Parents

_____

_____

Wishes for Baby

_____

_____

Guest

_____

My Predictions

Baby's date of birth					Time of birth					Hours of labor

Baby weight					Baby height

Hair color					Eye color

Name suggestion					First word

Advice for Parents

_____
_____

Wishes for Baby

_____
_____

Guest

My Predictions

Baby's date of birth

Time of birth

Hours of labor

Baby weight

Baby height

Hair color

Eye color

Name suggestion

First word

Advice for Parents

Wishes for Baby

Guest

My Predictions

Baby's date of birth

Time of birth

Hours of labor

Baby weight

Baby height

Hair color

Eye color

Name suggestion

First word

Advice for Parents

Wishes for Baby

Guest

My Predictions

Baby's date of birth	Time of birth	Hours of labor

Baby weight	Baby height

Hair color	Eye color

Name suggestion	First word

Advice for Parents

Wishes for Baby

Guest

My Predictions

Baby's date of birth

Time of birth

Hours of labor

Baby weight

Baby height

Hair color

Eye color

Name suggestion

First word

Advice for Parents

Wishes for Baby

Guest

My Predictions

Baby's date of birth   Time of birth   Hours of labor

Baby weight   Baby height

Hair color   Eye color

Name suggestion   First word

Advice for Parents

Wishes for Baby

Guest

My Predictions

Baby's date of birth

Time of birth

Hours of labor

Baby weight

Baby height

Hair color

Eye color

Name suggestion

First word

Advice for Parents

Wishes for Baby

Guest

My Predictions

Baby's date of birth

Time of birth

Hours of labor

Baby weight

Baby height

Hair color

Eye color

Name suggestion

First word

Advice for Parents

Wishes for Baby

Guest

My Predictions

Baby's date of birth

Time of birth

Hours of labor

Baby weight

Baby height

Hair color

Eye color

Name suggestion

First word

Advice for Parents

Wishes for Baby

Guest

My Predictions

Baby's date of birth   Time of birth   Hours of labor

Baby weight   Baby height

Hair color   Eye color

Name suggestion   First word

Advice for Parents

Wishes for Baby

Guest

My Predictions

Baby's date of birth

Time of birth

Hours of labor

Baby weight

Baby height

Hair color

Eye color

Name suggestion

First word

Advice for Parents

Wishes for Baby

Guest

My Predictions

Baby's date of birth   Time of birth   Hours of labor

Baby weight   Baby height

Hair color   Eye color

Name suggestion   First word

Advice for Parents

Wishes for Baby

Guest

My Predictions

Baby's date of birth

Time of birth

Hours of labor

Baby weight

Baby height

Hair color

Eye color

Name suggestion

First word

Advice for Parents

Wishes for Baby

Guest

My Predictions

Baby's date of birth   Time of birth   Hours of labor

Baby weight   Baby height

Hair color   Eye color

Name suggestion   First word

Advice for Parents

Wishes for Baby

Guest

My Predictions

Baby's date of birth

Time of birth

Hours of labor

Baby weight

Baby height

Hair color

Eye color

Name suggestion

First word

Advice for Parents

Wishes for Baby

Guest

My Predictions

Baby's date of birth   Time of birth   Hours of labor

Baby weight   Baby height

Hair color   Eye color

Name suggestion   First word

Advice for Parents

Wishes for Baby

Guest

My Predictions

Baby's date of birth

Time of birth

Hours of labor

Baby weight

Baby height

Hair color

Eye color

Name suggestion

First word

Advice for Parents

Wishes for Baby

Guest

My Predictions

Baby's date of birth

Time of birth

Hours of labor

Baby weight

Baby height

Hair color

Eye color

Name suggestion

First word

Advice for Parents

Wishes for Baby

Guest

My Predictions

Baby's date of birth

Time of birth

Hours of labor

Baby weight

Baby height

Hair color

Eye color

Name suggestion

First word

Advice for Parents

Wishes for Baby

Guest

_____

My Predictions

Baby's date of birth   Time of birth   Hours of labor

Baby weight   Baby height

Hair color   Eye color

Name suggestion   First word

Advice for Parents

_____
_____

Wishes for Baby

_____
_____

Guest

My Predictions

Baby's date of birth

Time of birth

Hours of labor

Baby weight

Baby height

Hair color

Eye color

Name suggestion

First word

Advice for Parents

Wishes for Baby

Guest

_____

My Predictions

Baby's date of birth   Time of birth   Hours of labor

Baby weight   Baby height

Hair color   Eye color

Name suggestion   First word

Advice for Parents

_____

_____

Wishes for Baby

_____

_____

Guest

My Predictions

Baby's date of birth

Time of birth

Hours of labor

Baby weight

Baby height

Hair color

Eye color

Name suggestion

First word

Advice for Parents

Wishes for Baby

Guest

_____

My Predictions

Baby's date of birth   Time of birth   Hours of labor

Baby weight   Baby height

Hair color   Eye color

Name suggestion   First word

Advice for Parents

_____
_____

Wishes for Baby

_____
_____

Guest

My Predictions

Baby's date of birth

Time of birth

Hours of labor

Baby weight

Baby height

Hair color

Eye color

Name suggestion

First word

Advice for Parents

Wishes for Baby

Guest

My Predictions

Baby's date of birth   Time of birth   Hours of labor

Baby weight   Baby height

Hair color   Eye color

Name suggestion   First word

Advice for Parents

Wishes for Baby

Guest

My Predictions

Baby's date of birth

Time of birth

Hours of labor

Baby weight

Baby height

Hair color

Eye color

Name suggestion

First word

Advice for Parents

_____

_____

Wishes for Baby

_____

_____

Guest

My Predictions

Baby's date of birth   Time of birth   Hours of labor

Baby weight   Baby height

Hair color   Eye color

Name suggestion   First word

Advice for Parents

Wishes for Baby

Guest

My Predictions

Baby's date of birth

Time of birth

Hours of labor

Baby weight

Baby height

Hair color

Eye color

Name suggestion

First word

Advice for Parents

Wishes for Baby

Guest

My Predictions

Baby's date of birth   Time of birth   Hours of labor

Baby weight   Baby height

Hair color   Eye color

Name suggestion   First word

Advice for Parents

Wishes for Baby

Guest

My Predictions

Baby's date of birth

Time of birth

Hours of labor

Baby weight

Baby height

Hair color

Eye color

Name suggestion

First word

Advice for Parents

Wishes for Baby

Guest

My Predictions

Baby's date of birth

Time of birth

Hours of labor

Baby weight

Baby height

Hair color

Eye color

Name suggestion

First word

Advice for Parents

Wishes for Baby

Guest

My Predictions

Baby's date of birth

Time of birth

Hours of labor

Baby weight

Baby height

Hair color

Eye color

Name suggestion

First word

Advice for Parents

Wishes for Baby

Guest

My Predictions

Baby's date of birth

Time of birth

Hours of labor

Baby weight

Baby height

Hair color

Eye color

Name suggestion

First word

Advice for Parents

Wishes for Baby

Guest

My Predictions

Baby's date of birth

Time of birth

Hours of labor

Baby weight

Baby height

Hair color

Eye color

Name suggestion

First word

Advice for Parents

Wishes for Baby

Guest

My Predictions

Baby's date of birth

Time of birth

Hours of labor

Baby weight

Baby height

Hair color

Eye color

Name suggestion

First word

Advice for Parents

Wishes for Baby

Gift Log

Gifts

Gift	Given By	Thank you note sent

Gifts

Gift	Given By	Thank you note sent

Gifts

Gift	Given By	Thank you note sent

Gifts

Gift	Given By	Thank you note sent

Gifts

Gift	Given By	Thank you note sent

Gifts

Gift	Given By	Thank you note sent

Gifts

Gift	Given By	Thank you note sent

Gifts

Gift	Given By	Thank you note sent

Gifts

Gift	Given By	Thank you note sent

Gifts

Gift	Given By	Thank you note sent

Made in United States
Orlando, FL
08 April 2023